Everyday Citizenship

Seven keys
to a life well lived

Wendy Perez and Simon Duffy

Illustrated by
Ester Ortega

Edited by
Clare Tarling

We are all equal.
We are all different.
We are all citizens.

Red Press
Everyday Citizenship: Seven keys to a life well lived
Wendy Perez and Simon Duffy

Printed and bound in the UK by CPI Group (UK)
Typeset in FS Me

Published by Red Press
Paperback ISBN: 9781912157228
Ebook ISBN: 9781912157235

A catalogue record for this book is available from the British Library

Red Press registered address:
6 Courtenay Close, Wareham, Dorset, BH20 4ED, England

redpress.co.uk | @redpresspub | #EverydayCitizenship

This book is dedicated
to our much-missed friend, Carl Poll
Founder of KeyRing

What's inside?

What's inside?

Hello!

My name is Wendy. I am a person with a learning disability and I live my life to the fullest.

I was always told I would not be able to do anything; but I got tired of hearing that.
I proved people wrong.

Simon Duffy's book, *Keys to Citizenship*, gave people who run social care services lots of ideas about how to do things differently.

When his book was published in 2003, a lively global community formed. People started using the keys in lots of different ways to make their lives better.

That inspired me to write this book with Simon. We worked equally as a team to give everyone ideas about citizenship, not just professionals.

I make choices about my life that are right for me. I have my own flat and my own company. I help people with learning disabilities have more control over their lives.

I am confident and I am independent. I have travelled around the world on my own. I know when I am taking risks and I take responsibility for them.

I do this to change people's attitudes and show them that they can do it too.

I wrote the stories in this book to show people how to start holding the keys to their own lives, with the right support.

Follow your dream, then people will believe in you from the start and help you along your path.

No dream is too small or too big. See what you can achieve, and don't ever stop!

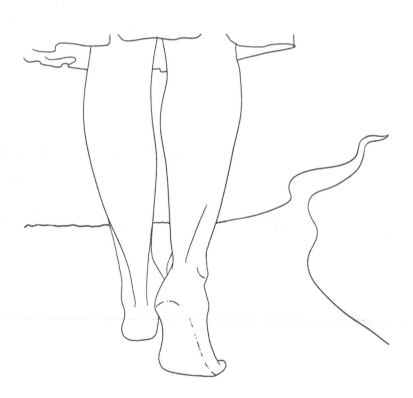

About this book

Each chapter presents one key to a life well lived, the life of a citizen. It explains what the key means and why it is important. It also has:

1. Things to try
A list of ideas, suggestions and reminders about each key

2. Warning signs
If you feel one or more of these things, something in your life might need to change

3. Wendy's story
An example from Wendy's life

What is citizenship?

Citizens matter

Your life

You can have a good life. Each of us brings something valuable into the world. All of us can have a life well lived.

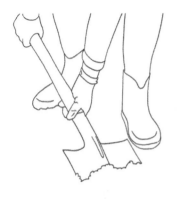

Our communities

Citizens take part in the life of the community. We all need friends and people who help us. We can all do something to help other people.

Our world

Citizens work to make the world a better place for everyone. We work together to change things and to make sure everyone is included and can lead a good life.

Everyone is a citizen

We don't need language or qualifications. We don't need to be the same as everyone else. We need everyone to be unique and different.

In a fair society, everyone can be a full citizen. Everyone is valued. Everyone is included. Everyone works together.

What citizens need

Citizens need rights

This includes getting the help we need to be a citizen.

Citizens need duties

This includes the duty to help others to be citizens.

Citizens need freedom

We live our own life, our own way, as part of a community.

Citizenship means a life well lived

'Citizenship is important because it means being treated with respect and dignity. Citizens are both equal and different.'

- Simon

'Citizenship means being part of everyday life, not being stuck in a box.'

- Wendy

'Why is it still so hard for people with learning disabilities who just want to do ordinary things for themselves?'

- *Wendy*

'Not only can people with disabilities be citizens, they're often the best citizens there are.'

- *Simon*

The seven keys

Everyone is a citizen.

It doesn't matter what body or gifts you're born with. Everyone can have a life well lived.

Everyday citizenship is a life with:

1. Meaning

Enjoy life and make a difference.

2. Freedom

Take charge of your own life.

3. Money

Get the money you need to live.

4. Help

Get good help from other people.

5. Home

Find a place where you belong.

6. Community

Take part in the life of your community.

7. Love

Enjoy friendship, love and family.

1. Meaning

Enjoy life and make a difference.

Citizens have meaningful lives. They have a sense of purpose.

Sometimes finding a sense of purpose comes naturally. You already know what you want to achieve.

Other times, we don't know what our purpose in life is.

This can happen when other people take control, exploit us or boss us around. You might feel trapped or stuck.

There are ways to break out of this feeling.

Here are things to try:

1. Dare to dream

It may be difficult to believe that life can be better.

Your ideas about the future may seem silly or impossible.

Achieving even a small part of your dream may help you find the hope you need to build a better life.

Think about your goals as a series of small, manageable steps. This will help you tackle each one.

Notice your progress, and celebrate it!

2. Connect with people

People can help you to do new things.

Find people who believe in you, even when you don't believe in yourself.

3. Have faith in your gifts

You have many gifts and talents. More than anyone can count.

Use, share and enjoy your gifts. It is not selfish to think about yourself. You have knowledge and experience that will help other people.

4. Join in

There are lots of places where you will be welcomed.

You can enjoy yourself and make friends.

5. Get a job

It may seem difficult, but working and volunteering are great ways of meeting people. You will learn, make friends and do useful things.

A paid job means you can earn some extra money. Money can help with other parts of your life.

Here are some warning signs:

Forgetting that you have talents, skills and gifts.

Wasting your time, talents or money.

Thinking that no one cares about you.

Feeling cut off, isolated and unable to join in.

Losing hope and not believing that things can get better.

'Sometimes people are encouraged to make a plan for absolutely everything. I got fed up with that. I only plan for big things now. With the little things, I just take life as it comes, like everyone else.'

- Wendy

Wendy's story:

Having a paid job matters to me; I am worth it!

I like making a difference to people's lives by doing consultancy and training. I like to help people plan ahead.

At work, I am with people who think like me: people who listen and are open-minded. I love being part of a team.

I started like anyone else: I filled in an application form. At the interview, I was the only person with a learning disability.

The government provided some support to help me work. But the best people to support me with the work itself are my colleagues.

I have lots of ideas, and we work together to develop products and training programmes. So when I work, the customer gets what they want, my employer gets what they want and I get what I want.

There is no difference between me and any other member of staff. We all have our own skills and talents. We are equal, but not the same!

All organisations should employ people with different abilities and skills. It works!

I have learned this: do not just say you are going to do things; start today! Action is louder than words.

2. Freedom

Take charge of your own life.

Citizens are free...

...but sometimes freedom is lost.

People with disabilities often find that other people take control of their lives.

It is especially hard for people who do not use words to communicate.

Here are things to try:

1. Remember you're in charge

You have the right to be in control of your own life.

2. Learn about your options

Talk to other people about what works well for them. Find out what is happening in your neighbourhood.

3. Use your voice

Learn to speak your mind. Get help from people you trust to speak out.

4. Ask people to listen

It's important to find people in your life who value your ideas and listen to you with an open mind.

5. Get help to make things happen

You might need help to express your thoughts and make sure other people take your decisions seriously.

Different groups and people can give practical help to put your plan into action.

Here are some warning signs:

Other people making decisions for you.

Being unable to tell people what you want.

Not knowing your options and just accepting what happens.

People not knowing how to communicate with you.

Nothing gets done, things just keep going round in circles.

Wendy's story:

I worked at an organisation called Paradigm, and I had a team event in Amsterdam. There was a big storm on the day I travelled.

The wind was howling. Some of my team travelled earlier, in better weather. Some decided to stay home.

Everyone told me not to go.

I went on the plane on my own. It was a big risk, but I proved that I could do it.

I arrived at the hotel and my team was shocked to see me!

I said; 'You don't know me well enough! I like to take a risk and see what I am capable of. Have more faith in me.'

But the truth was I had been very scared.

3. Money

Get the money you need to live.

As a citizen, you need enough money to live with dignity and security.

Too many people, especially citizens with disabilities, live in poverty. Not having enough money makes things hard.

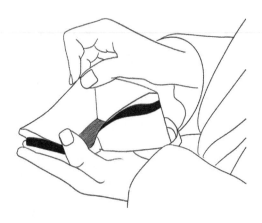

Here are things to try:

1. Know your rights

Make sure you get everything you are entitled to:

- services
- benefits
- discounts.

Getting good advice on your rights is important.

2. Look for paid work

People you know may have ideas. Volunteering can sometimes lead to paid work.

Look at websites or your local newspaper.

Your local college may help you get qualifications.

3. Be flexible

Decide how to get the best out your money. Sometimes you don't need more, you just need to be creative about how you use it.

Personal budgets can give you more choice about paying for any support you need.

A personal budget is extra money to pay for the things you may need to live.

4. Get help and advice

It is useful to get help to manage your money. Ask a financial adviser, a friend, or someone you can trust.

You might need help with big decisions, or with everyday budgeting.

5. Set aside savings

We all need savings: money to use in emergencies, for a holiday or even a home.

Save what you can each week.

Use a bank account that is separate from your everyday money.

Here are some warning signs:

Not getting the benefits and help you are entitled to.

Being afraid to take risks and to earn your own money.

Putting up with choices that other people make for you.

People taking advantage, using your money as if it were theirs. This is very serious: get help!

Being afraid of having no savings to use in emergencies.

Wendy's story:

Mum set up a bank account for me. I wanted to take control of the account, so we went to the bank.

The cashier asked whether I could sign for my own money when they saw that I use a wheelchair!

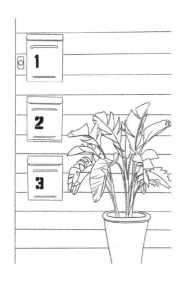

Mum and I filled in the form and spoke to the manager. The cashier got told off for nearly turning away a good customer.

Now I have four bank accounts:

- personal money
- savings
- personal budget
- business.

4. Help

Get good help from other people.

The best kind of help is invisible. People know when to step in and step out. They give you the chance to think and try for things yourself.

We all need help. Lots of the help you receive you won't even notice. Good help makes you stronger, but bad help harms you.

People with disabilities might need extra help, but sometimes others help too much. They forget you are a citizen and you are in control of your own life.

Here are things to try:

1. Do what matters to you

Good help gives you what you need to achieve your plans. You might get help to do activities like going to the gym. It might be help from friends or family.

2. Keep learning

Getting the right help means you can keep learning and making the most of your abilities.

3. Make new friends

Don't be afraid to build new friendships and connections. Good help encourages you to meet new people and to work with others.

4. Work as equals

Good help is respectful, it is given in a spirit of equality and mutual benefit. Working together benefits everyone.

5. Find a champion

Good help means having someone to look out for you. Everyone needs someone who can stick up for us sometimes.

Here are some warning signs:

People not helping you do what is important to you. They try to control everything.

Feeling weak and dependent on others.

Feeling segregated and cut out of ordinary life.

The person offering help is just wrong for you.

People abusing their power as a helper.

Wendy's story:

In December 2000, I applied for a personal budget. A personal budget is the extra money to pay for the things you may need to live as an equal citizen.

I wanted to be in control of my life, like everyone else. I knew I needed extra support, but it had to be flexible.

The care agency supporting me didn't understand that a person with a learning disability can have a job. They thought that I should stay at home instead of travelling for work or going out to see friends in the evening.

I decided to use some of my personal budget to employ personal assistants to help me with things I couldn't do by myself. It is really important for me that I can work with people I like and trust. Life changes all the time and you need to be flexible.

When you get a personal budget you can still get help to manage it. Family or friends can help or there are organisations who will organise and provide the extra help you need. Before, I used a payroll scheme to help me pay my support staff and now I use a service that employs my personal assistants for me.

Having a personal budget should help put you in control of your life. If you don't like something, then you should be able to change it. If you can see a better way of doing things, then you can be creative and change how you use your budget. Most of all, personal budgets can help you get involved in the community doing the things that matter to you.

5. Home

Find a place where you belong.

Citizens belong. You are an equal member of the community with your neighbours, friends and family.

You should have a home where you are safe in a community that is right for you.

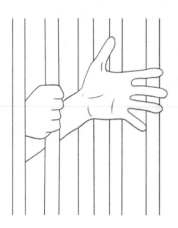

Many people with disabilities find themselves living with their families for too long, or stuck in care homes.

Here are things to try:

1. Find a place to be yourself

A good home has privacy so you can unwind and do your own thing.

2. Find a place where you belong

It is important you live in a place where you feel comfortable and are valued by the people around you.

3. Welcome your loved ones

You should be able to invite your neighbours, friends and family into your home any time you want to.

4. Always be safe

You should be able to live with people you like and never live in fear.

5. Know your rights

You should have strong rights and should not have to worry about losing your home.

Here are some warning signs:

Lacking privacy. You might not be free to do your own thing, get grumpy or let off steam.

Living far away from family and friends. Living in a place you didn't choose.

Being shut off or locked in. Being unable to invite people to visit.

Living with people you didn't choose to live with, or with people you don't like or who abuse you.

Lacking housing rights, with no control over your future.

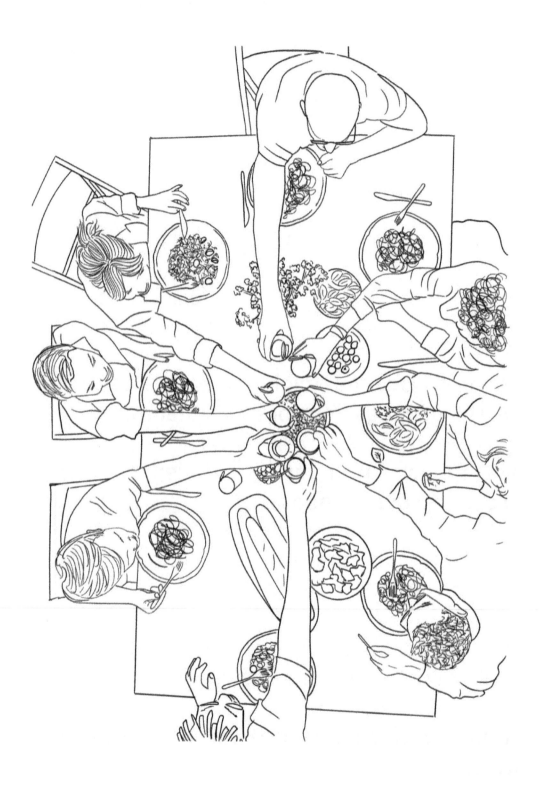

Wendy's story:

I did all the same things as other children when I was growing up. Mum wanted us to live the same sort of life as other families. She wanted me to be myself, and to learn things by doing them. I still live that way.

Friends always came to our home. They still do! We often went out as a family and always went on holiday in the summer. We would talk about where to go, and plan it all together. For many people with learning disabilities, life is not like this.

Mum and Dad sometimes left me at home on my own, because they trusted me. They let me become an independent adult. Having a good life at home, with the support of my family, made everything else possible.

I moved out of my parents' home when I was 27. It was hard, but it was the right time. I put my name on the housing list. I found a flat and I am still here.

I moved house step by step. I had great support. To start with, I spent three days at my parents' home and then three days in my flat.

Using care agencies didn't work for me. They only thought about my support needs, not about me as a whole person. That is why I got a personal budget. It means I have more control.

My personal budget is given to me as a direct payment. It's money I spend on support. To decide how to use it wisely, I had to think about what I like doing, what help I need and I want in the future.

Simon has worked to show that everybody can live in their own home. He created an organisation called Inclusion Glasgow to support people with very complex disabilities to live in their own homes with support organised around their needs.

From my own experience and the training I have given people, I know that living on your own with the right support is possible. Try it if you want to. It worked for me!

6. Community

Take part in the life of your community.

Community starts around you. You are not alone. Make a positive difference to your community. It is part of being a citizen.

Family is community. You were born into a family. It can be one of the most important sources of love in your life.

Friends are community. You need friends. You can live alongside people and make friends all through your life.

Neighbours are community. When you belong in a place, your neighbours can be people you help and who help you.

Jobs are community. You can make new friends at work. Work is a way to help other people.

Interests create community. If you are interested in something, join up with other people to do it. You can meet people at places of worship, craft groups, fitness classes, sports clubs and many other places.

Here are things to try:

1. Join in

You will find lots happening in your community if you look. Try looking at noticeboards, the local paper and social media to find things you are interested in. Ask around, look around, and even ask your phone.

2. Find work

A supportive workplace can be a very close community. Remember that a job interview is your chance to find out if it is the right place for you, so use that time to ask questions.

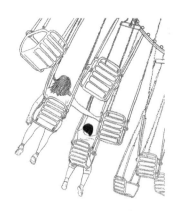

3. Have fun

Find places where you are happy, can laugh, relax and have fun.

4. Enjoy togetherness

Being part of the community is how you meet other people and make friends. Ask people for help when you need it, and help other people too.

5. Grow your power

Work with other people to help make positive changes to your community and the world. Together you can achieve so much more than on your own.

Here are some warning signs:

Finding that you're living without purpose and feeling bored.

Feeling like you're not valued by others because nobody knows what you can do.

Ending up in services that are just poor imitations of ordinary life.

Feeling like it is hard to make friends. This makes you feel weaker, lonelier, and that your options are limited.

Wendy's story:

There's a world out there. Get involved, even if it feels risky at first. One of my big passions is football and supporting Arsenal.

I was interested in football from the age of five, even before I could talk and walk. I've had my own season ticket since 2003. The football club gives me an extra membership card for the person who supports me on the day.

Since I have been going to see Arsenal, people have seen the change in me and see me as me. But we're all different. Not everyone loves football and not everyone loves Arsenal (especially Simon, who is a Bolton Wanderers fan).

What does community life look like for you? A good place to start is to think about what you enjoy and what you want to get out of being part of a community.

My friend, Carl Poll, believed in the gifts of people with learning disabilities. He created KeyRing, a system of neighbourhood networks where people with learning disabilities help each other to live independently in the community.

There are things you can join as a member, help or volunteer with. There are jobs you can apply for. There are people you can ask to help or connect you. You have a right to be part of the community, and the community needs you and your gifts.

7. Love

Enjoy friendship, love and family.

When we love someone we want them to have a life of citizenship. And a life of citizenship should be a life full of love.

Love makes everything possible, and everything worthwhile.

Here are things to try:

1. Love who you are

Know your strengths. Love and be proud of who you are. You deserve to be treated with respect by other people.

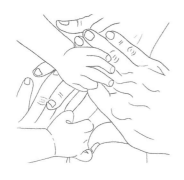

2. Love your family

You can be part of a family. You have the legal right to have a private family life.

3. Love your friends

You can find real friends, people who value you for who you really are.

4. Love your lovers

You are a full human being who should be allowed to have affection and sex if you and your partner both want to.

5. Love the world

You have unique gifts to share. You can find your way to make the world a better place.

Here are some warning signs:

Being abused, made to have sex or be hurt in other ways.

Losing your family or being told not to have children.

Having no real friends, even when you are surrounded by other people.

Missing out on sex and the chance to be someone's lover.

Being closed off, unwilling to love, frightened of giving your gifts to the world.

Wendy's story:

I read Simon's book, *Keys to Citizenship*. I liked how it inspired people to ask for the things they really wanted but were scared to talk about. It gave people courage. It described the way I live my life: as a citizen.

But I saw two problems with the book: it didn't include the voices of people with learning disabilities, and it didn't talk about relationships or sex.

People should know that they have a right to relationships, and they might need help to learn about sex.

Knowledge helps to protect us from abuse, even if it's embarrassing to talk about.

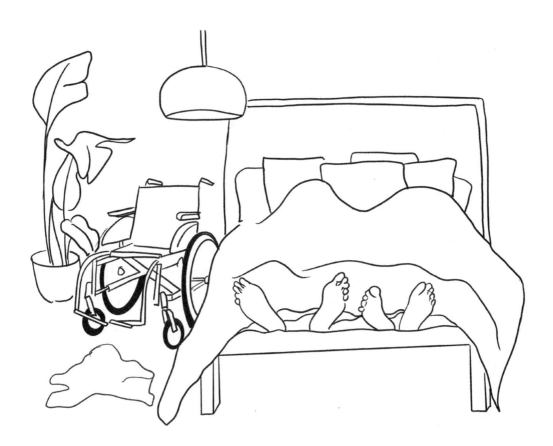

I found out how frightened people are to talk about sex when I worked on an Easy Read book about it.

We used illustrations to make it clear what sex was. People with learning disabilities said the pictures really helped them.

Love isn't always about romantic love; it isn't always about sex. It can be about friendships with people who believe in you; people who will go the extra mile for you.

When I was small, life was hard because I could not talk. I couldn't say what I needed to say, even though I had it in my head. Some teachers didn't want to spend the extra time to help me. They planned to send me away to a residential school.

But with love and support from my family and friends I was constantly included in the life of my community. Sometimes I have had to fight for that too, so some people say I am a loud-mouth, but nobody can stop me. I work, I wrote this book, I try to make society better. I have done more than anyone ever thought was possible, all because of love.

What next?

Start your citizenship journey

This book is full of practical wisdom and insight to help you live a life of meaning. It asks you the right questions to help you find your own answers.

But it's only the beginning: the real journey to citizenship lies ahead.

Let's change the world by becoming the best citizens we can be!

Join Citizen Network

You are a citizen and you deserve a life well lived. The seven keys show you how to achieve that.

Yet sometimes there are barriers to citizenship:

- unfair laws that don't give you the rights you need
- prejudices that stop people seeing you for who you really are
- not having the power you need.

Citizen Network is a global community to support a world where everyone matters, inspired by the seven keys.

You can join Citizen Network for free. You can find information and ideas to help you, and use the map to find member organisations near you. Find out more at **citizen-network.org**.

There's also a community within Citizen Network of people using the seven keys to citizenship model in interesting ways. Find out more at **keystocitizenship.com**.

Share your ideas and stories

Tell a friend about this book, and share your learning with them.

Join or create a group to work together with other people to be everyday citizens.

Celebrate acts of everyday citizenship by others by sharing positive stories from your community.

If you share stories on social media, use the hashtag #EverydayCitizenship and we'll share it too!

Keep learning about your options

Simon's book, *Keys to Citizenship*, had practical advice about support, housing, money and other issues.

Now, most of this information is available online or through the right groups and organisations.

Remember that things vary by region, by country, and over time.

Keep learning about your options and connect with useful organisations near you. Here are some terms to search for online:

1. Meaning

Ask yourself questions about what is important to you or get help from someone to develop your life plan.

Search for: Person Centred Planning, PATH, MAPS, Essential Lifestyle Planning, Now & Next Alumni, Support Planning, Inclusion

2. Freedom

You may need help to express yourself, learn about your options or organise things.

Search for: Easy Read, Supported Decision-Making, Self-Advocacy, Facilitated Communication, Support Brokerage

3. Money

Find out what you're entitled to. With the right help, most people can do paid work.

Search for: Supported Employment, Welfare Rights, Disability Benefits, Universal Basic Income, Basic Income Plus, Job Coach, Training in Systematic Instruction

4. Help

Get help to do the things you really want to, how and when you want to.

Search for: Peer Support, Personal Assistant, Personal Budget, Self-Directed Support, Individual Service Fund, Personal Assistance, Self-Managed Funding, Direct Payments, Natural Support

5. Home

Whether you're renting or buying, find somewhere that is safe, private and right for you.

Search for: Flatmates, Support Tenants, Supportive Flatmates, Supported Living, Home Ownership, Shared Ownership, Accessible Housing

6. Community

If you want to take part in your community, the best place to start is often your own neighbourhood.

Search for: Inclusive Education, Asset-Based Community Development, Local Area Coordination, Community Mapping, Neighbourhood Democracy

7. Love

You need love in its many forms. You also need to make sure you are safe and free from exploitation. Add "+ Learning Disability" after any of these terms to find good information.

Search for: Supported Loving, Sex Education, Relationship

Our team

About the authors

Wendy Perez

Wendy is a leading disability activist, and does consultancy through her organisation, See Me As Me.

At Paradigm, Wendy trained people with disabilities and their families on independent living, personal budgets and support plans.

She helped develop important government policy on services for people with learning disabilties.

For St George's Hospital, Wendy trained medical students to meet the needs of people with learning disabilities.

Wendy co-authored a chapter in *Learning Disability Today* and a number of books in the *Books Beyond Words* series. She has contributed to Mencap's newsletter, *Viewpoint*.

Wendy lives in London. She is an avid Arsenal supporter, Mac user and DJs under the name "Hotwheels".

Wendy is proud to live as a citizen, showing that people with disabilities can live full and positive lives, under their own control. She always wants to try new things.

Wendy helped create Citizen Network and now works as part of the team to provide training on everyday citizenship.

Simon Duffy

Simon is a philosopher working for a world where everyone matters. For over 30 years he's helped people with learning disabilities take their place as full citizens.

Simon founded Inclusion Glasgow to provide individualised support to people with complex disabilities. In Sheffield, he worked to encourage local and central government to adopt the idea of self-directed support.

After helping create Citizen Network, Simon works on growing new forms of action to create the world we need in the face of climate breakdown and species extinction. He helped start the UBI Lab Network that advocates for economic security a guaranteed basic income for everyone. He helped start the Neighbourhood Democracy Movement that advocates for meaningful democratic action in every community.

Today, Simon is President of Citizen Network and Director of Citizen Network Research. Simon also has a doctorate in philosophy and continues to write about theology, ethics and social justice.

He is a proud citizen of Sheffield and loves to spend time with his family in the garden and the countryside.

About the illustrator

Ester Ortega

Ester is an artist-activist. She works at the Fundación Inclusión y Apoyo Aprocor. In 2007. She co-founded "Debajo del Sombrero", using art to challenge the institutionalisation of people with learning disabilities.

About the editor

Clare Tarling

Clare is a freelance Easy Read designer who loves disability advocacy, information accessibility and exciting new collaborations. She has over 20 years' experience designing for museums, the NHS, charities and local authorities.

See Me As Me

Wendy Perez's company (See Me as Me) does training and talks on *Everyday Citizenship*. She talks with people with learning disabilities, families and professionals about why citizenship really matters.

Wendy will share ideas from the book, stories from her own life and examples of good practice from around the world.

Learn more here: **see-me-as-me.co.uk**.